Releasing the Cry Within
Life is Worth Living

By
Katina Scott

Published By: Tamika INK

Library of Congress Cataloging-in-Publication Data has been applied for

ISBN:

PRINTED IN THE UNITED STATES OF AMERICA

Table of Contents

O ne day, it all came to an end, and I found myself wondering, "What do I do now?" I found myself in a place where although there was life inside me, I didn't want to live. I thought, "What am I supposed to do; how do I go on? God, help me. No, wait! Did you let this happen to me? How could you let this happen? Where are you, God? Why do I feel so alone? Is anybody listening? Don't they see that I need help? How can they just ignore me? What's wrong with me? Why can't someone love me? God, it hurts so much. When is the pain just going to end?"

Does this sound familiar? Have you ever asked yourself any of these questions? I know, my sister, that somewhere you are out there and you have or are asking these very same questions. I want to encourage you; don't give up. Even though you don't understand, God is still there, and He is working on your behalf.

My prayer is that as you go through this book, you will spend some quiet time with the Lord and allow Him to speak to your heart. On the journal pages after each section, take a few minutes and write down those things that the Lord whispered to you during your time with Him. I promise that if you are still and stay in His presence long enough, He will speak. All you have to do is listen and obey!

CHAPTER ONE

believe that God allows things to happen in our life because, first and foremost, He has to establish who is number one. I grew up in the church, and going to church every Sunday was a part of my life. But, actually letting God be the head of my life was something I was not familiar with. The Word of God says that we have a form of godliness but deny the power thereof, (2 Timothy 3:5, King James Version). I could feel that my life was changing. I was introduced to the Holy Spirit, and I didn't know exactly what was happening. When I went to church, it was not just church, as usual. You see, God had a plan for me, but I did not understand. My husband was the most important person in this world to me, even though I tried to convince myself that was not true. But looking back, He definitely was. When you do things just to please someone else or compromise your beliefs for someone else, you are putting them above your God.

In Exodus 20:3-5, God clearly states that we shall not have any other gods before Him and that He is a jealous God.

It mattered more to me what my husband was going to say about something than what God was going to say. God has to be our first choice. He is not going to settle for second best in any situation. How would you feel to know that your husband really wanted to marry your best friend, but she turned Him down, so he settled for you? Well, isn't that what we do to God? We *settle* for Him because the person that we really want is not there. God has to be first. We have to have a personal relationship with Him. Our life depends on it.

Each morning I make a conscious decision to recognize God first. Would you like to do this as well? Make a decision to start right now.

Prayer Starter

Lord Jesus, I invite you into my life. I declare with my mouth that Jesus is Lord and believe with my heart that you raised Him from the dead. I accept you into my life and make you my Lord and Savior. I speak now that I give you first priority in my life now and forever.

Devotional Scriptures

Psalms 42:1-2

As the deer pants for streams of water, so my soul pants for
you. My soul thirsts for God, for the living God.
(New International Version)

Psalms 63:1-1

O God of my life, I'm lovesick for you in this weary wilderness.
I thirst with the deepest longings to love you more, with
cravings in my heart that can't be described.
Such yearning grips my soul for you, my God!
(Passion Translation)

Psalms 143:8

Cause me to hear thy lovingkindness in the morning; for in
thee do I trust: cause me to know the way wherein I should
walk; for I lift up my soul unto thee. (King James Version)

Reflection Questions

1. When you wake up in the morning, what is the first thing you think about?

   _____

   _____

   _____

   _____

   _____

2. When times get hard, who are you turning to for help? Do you find yourself calling friends, your significant other, family, etc. Or do you go to God first?)

   _____

   _____

   _____

   _____

   _____

3. What can you do to make sure that God is your number one source?

   _____

   _____

   _____

Journal

_____

_____

_____

_____

_____

_____

_____

_____

_____

_____

_____

_____

_____

_____

_____

_____

_____

_____

_____

_____

_____

_____

CHAPTER TWO

Why So Much Pain-Finding My Way From Death To Life

My heart felt like it had been stabbed over and over again. I thought there was nothing that could ever make the pain stop. I didn't understand why my Father who loves me so much, who wants me to prosper and be in good health even as my soul prospers, who has a plan for my life, would do this to me?

"Why?" I screamed this every day. I asked the question "Lord, do you know what you're doing?"

Have you ever felt like you were just existing but not living? Like you were just going through the motions in life, asking yourself, "What happened? How did I get to this point?"

Every day suicide would come to visit me, and I would consider it more and more. It felt like all hope was gone. No one loves me; no one cares, why go on? Here I was at the point of not wanting to keep my own life but amazingly enough; I had life growing inside of me. Now, I realize that the life growing inside of me helped to save my life.

I would like to pause for a minute and be honest and confess that this was not just a few days or weeks before deliverance came, but for me it was a few years. I believe that God is now doing a quick work in the earth. So, I wanted to share my story with you so that you could be delivered in a moment! We no longer have years to get ourselves together. Before my deliverance, I kept living and moving for my children. They were the only reasons that I kept going on. I remember hearing God say, "I am here for you." But why would I go to Him? He had let me down.

The first thing that God said to me to bring deliverance in my life was, *"God is not a man."*

What does that mean? Why was that so important to me? In Numbers 23:19, it states that God is not a man that he should lie nor the Son of man that he should repent. I found that I kept putting God in the same category as every man in my life that had ever hurt me. My first significant memory of my childhood is my mother telling me that my Father had gone to live with another woman. I was about four or five years old. This continued for the rest of my childhood with my Father coming in and out of my life. As a result, from an early age, I grew up thinking that a father wasn't always going to be there, and men could not be trusted. When my husband cheated on me and went on to do his own thing, it just fortified my convictions even more. Men were not to be trusted. Don't believe what they say; they are not telling the truth. They only want to use you; you'll just get hurt. These were the lies that kept playing in my head.

One Sunday after church, while walking outside to get into my car, I heard a voice saying to me, "But God is not a man!" I stopped dead in my tracks. For the first time, the lies were being canceled out by this truth in God's Word. God is not a man! He is the Father of us all. He is our Lord. He is or Savior. Almighty God sent His Son to die for us to redeem us from the sin curse that we were born into through Adam. He was born of a virgin so that he would remain pure. He bore our infirmities so He understands all our pain. God is not a man; He is the sovereign God. Please accept this truth so that you can go on. This is a truth, a key principle in our Christian walk. God is not a man! Glory! Aren't you glad of that? I know I was when I finally realized it. I had to take Him out of the category that I'd placed Him in and put Him in a class all by Himself. One of sovereignty, one of absoluteness, one of authority! Hallelujah!

Prayer Starter

Lord Jesus, I declare that you are not a man and will not hurt me as the other men in my life have. You are God and God alone. Thank you for not giving up on me even when I didn't trust you. Thank you for taking my broken heart that's in so many pieces and making me whole and new again. In Jesus' name!

Devotional Scriptures

Psalms 34:18

The Lord is nigh unto them that are of a broken heart; and saveth such as be of a contrite spirit. (Kings James Version)

Revelation 21:4

And God shall wipe away all tears from their eyes; and there shall be no more death, neither sorrow, nor crying, neither shall there be any more pain; for the former things are passed away. (King James Version)

Isaiah 41:10

Fear thou not; for I am with thee: be not dismayed for I am thy God: I will strengthen thee: yea, I will help thee; yea I will uphold thee with the right hand of my righteousness. (King James Version)

Reflection Questions

1. Think about a time when you were just existing and not living. When was it?

    _____

    _____

    _____

    _____

    _____

2. Are you ready to move past this point?

    _____

    _____

    _____

    _____

    _____

3. What lies do you need to get rid of to accept the truth of God's word?

    _____

    _____

    _____

    _____

    _____

Journal

_____

_____

_____

_____

_____

_____

_____

_____

_____

_____

_____

_____

_____

_____

_____

_____

_____

_____

_____

_____

CHAPTER THREE

What Is Love Anyway?

H ow loosely we use this four-letter word, LOVE. To so many of us, it is just a word. However, I would like to challenge you today by saying that until you allow God to love you, you haven't even experienced true love yet. No matter what I was feeling or how upset I was at God, He kept telling me how much He loved me. I kept asking, "Why?"

Do you know how low your self-esteem can get when you give everything to someone, and they just throw you and what you are giving them away? Until we realize that God loves us, we can never reach our full potential. God loves you. Everything that He did from the beginning of time he had you in mind all along. Jeremiah says that before you were in your mother's womb, I knew you; (Jeremiah 1:5). So, everything He has done was done with you, and you alone in mind. Who else can prove their love to you like that? Think about the circumstances that you have been through, you can hardly believe that you are still alive today, but you are because God loves you. He loves you so much that He gave His Son's life, (John 3:16), just to save you. Greater love hath no man than this than to lay down his life for his friends (John 15:13).

Who else in your life has proven their love to this degree? I haven't found a person on earth yet who loves me like this. God's love is so special and unique because even when we are trying to do everything except but what He is telling us to do, He is still there saying, "You are my daughter, and I love you. It doesn't matter what you've done; I love you. It doesn't matter what you're doing; I love you. It doesn't matter, what you're going to do, I love you. Just accept my love."

Unlike humans, God's love is not conditional, "If you do this or that for me, then I love you; but when you stop, the love stops."

Thank goodness, God is not like us. God loves us unconditionally. He loves us when we are giving Him what He wants and when we are blaming Him for everything. He never turns His back on us. It is us, His children, who turn away from Him, but God has never moved. In Malachi 3:6, it says that I the Lord changeth not. So, who changed in this love relationship? You or God?

<u>Prayer Starter</u>

Lord Jesus, in this journey of learning what love is, I give my heart to you, to love me, comfort me, change me from the inside out. I give myself to you.

Devotional Scriptures

John 3:16

For God so loved the world, that He gave His only begotten Son, that whosoever believeth in Him should not perish, but have everlasting life. (King James Version)

I John 4:18

There is no fear in love; but perfect love casteth out fear: because fear has torment. He that feareth is not made perfect in love. (King James Version)

John 15:13

Greater love hath no man than this, that a man lay down His life for His friends. (King James Version)

Reflection Questions

1. If you are being totally honest today, would you say that you love yourself?

    _____

    _____

    _____

    _____

    _____

2. Do you believe that God loves you?

    _____

    _____

    _____

    _____

    _____

3. Have you ever experienced the pure love of God?

    _____

    _____

    _____

    _____

    _____

Journal

_____

_____

_____

_____

_____

_____

_____

_____

_____

_____

_____

_____

_____

_____

_____

_____

_____

_____

_____

_____

_____

_____

CHAPTER FOUR

Who Says I Have To Forgive?

F orgiveness is an important component of emotional freedom and breakthrough. You must forgive whoever did you wrong. I know he hurt you so badly, so why should you just let him get away? I know you want him to pay for what he did. I know you want him to suffer; you're suffering, why shouldn't he?

Sometimes forgiveness is the last thing that we have on our mind. We say to ourselves that we will never be able to forgive him for what he did to us.

Well, my sister, I am here today to tell you that forgiving him is not an option; it is a must. You have to forgive to move on; to be healed yourself and to be totally free. Unforgiveness affects us in so many areas of our lives. Unforgiveness holds us captive, not the other person. In case you didn't notice they are going on with their lives. Unforgiveness causes you to miss out on God's promises for you. It can also cause physical ailments in your body.

Because forgiveness is a spiritual action, we must ask God to give us a mind and a heart to forgive so we can walk in freedom. The Word of God says that God will avenge; it is not up to us to get the person back. Luke 6:37 says that when we forgive others, then God will forgive us of our sins. So, stop praying for God to forgive you of your sins until you can forgive your transgressor. It honestly doesn't matter what someone does to us; God's Word still commands us to forgive them. Jesus gave us the perfect example of this when He was literally hanging on Calvary's cross, and says, "Father forgive them for they know not what they do."

I may be wrong, but I don't believe that we have been nailed to a cross. I have to repeat it; forgiveness is not an option; it is a must.

Prayer Starter

Lord Jesus, give me a heart and mind to forgive those who have hurt me. Lord, I desire to be free. Jesus, I lay them at your feet so that I may live and live abundantly.

Devotional Scriptures

Matthew 6:14

For if ye forgive men their trespasses, your heavenly father will also forgive you. (Kings James Version)

Colossians 3:13

Forbearing one another, and forgiving one another, if any man have a quarrel against any: even as Christ forgave you, so also do ye. (King James Version)

Luke 6:37

Judge not, and ye shall not be judged: condemn not, and ye shall not be condemned: forgive, and ye shall be forgiven (King James Version)

Reflection Questions:

1. Do you still get mad and upset when you think about what that person-(s) did to you?

   _____

   _____

   _____

   _____

   _____

2. Are you ready to totally let go of the hurt and pain?

   _____

   _____

   _____

   _____

   _____

3. Have you forgiven yourself?

   _____

   _____

   _____

   _____

   _____

Journal

_____

_____

_____

_____

_____

_____

_____

_____

_____

_____

_____

_____

_____

_____

_____

_____

_____

_____

_____

_____

_____

_____

_____

CHAPTER FIVE

Turn your tears of sorrow into tears of joy. , Understanding God's love is imperative for your recovery. Once you have the knowledge that God is not trying to kill you and that he does have a plan for your life (Jeremiah 29:11), God will begin to work on your heart. This is where God will start to dig away at your heart and tear down all the walls that you have built up. During life, we build up walls or shields for ourselves because we have been hurt so much by people who said they loved us. But in them loving us, we were beaten and bruised. So, we decided, "I'm not going to make myself vulnerable like that again."

We then start to build up walls, and subconsciously lock everyone and everything out. Oh, we fool ourselves and others because we do allow them to get to a certain point, but then the sensors go off that say they are getting too close, and we put up the stop sign again. Well, once we start believing that God loves us and we receive His love, He can then tear those walls down. We can begin to feel again. This is where we get rid of the Spirit of Fear, and we take on trust.

The Spirit of Fear has been a comfort to us for so long because the wall was not just one layer thick, but it was layers upon layers. Therefore, we now have to start saying to God, "I receive Your love."

The more we receive His love, we will begin to say goodbye to the Spirit of Fear. 2 Timothy 1:7 says, for God has not given us the Spirit of Fear, but love power and a sound mind.

God is telling us to trust Him. Taking one day at a time, 24 hours a day, trusting that God will provide that He will take care of us no matter what. We are no longer afraid of the world and being rejected and not wanted, because we are beginning to trust God enough that He will not leave us or forsake us. I promise that experiencing God's love is nothing like you've ever experienced before. I remember the first time that I had truly been intimate with God. It was an experience like none other. I had been with God and came out feeling pure and whole.

<u>*Prayer Starter*</u>

Lord Jesus, I give this fear over to you. I no longer want to be stuck in my past but want to move towards my future. Lord, help me to be free; I surrender to you.

Devotional Scriptures:

Deuteronomy 31:8

Do not be afraid or discouraged, for the LORD will personally go ahead of you. He will be with you; He will neither fail you nor abandon you." (New Living Translation)

2 Timothy 1:7

For God hath not given us the Spirit of fear and timidity, but of power, love and self-discipline (New Living Translation)

Psalms 34:4

I prayed to the Lord, and He answered me. He freed me from all my fears. (New Living Translation)

Reflection Questions

1. **Close your eyes, take a deep breath, what is it that you are really afraid of?**

    _____

    _____

    _____

    _____

    _____

2. **What is stopping you from turning your fear over to God?**

    _____

    _____

    _____

    _____

    _____

3. **What still makes you say, "God I know but....?"**

    _____

    _____

    _____

    _____

    _____

Journal

_____

_____

_____

_____

_____

_____

_____

_____

_____

_____

_____

_____

_____

_____

_____

_____

_____

_____

_____

_____

_____

_____

CHAPTER SIX

No More Pity Parties!

The crying stage in your life is over. Tears of sorrow, rejection, and "poor me" are now gone. It's amazing how knowing that someone loves you can change your life in an instant. Don't believe me? Remember when you were single and then all of a sudden you had someone interested in you. He pursued you and swept you off your feet with a few simple gestures and a few words. Your life changed in just a day. You began to make plans, think about your future, there's a skip in your step, and a smile is always on your face.

Well, how about when you realize that God is in love with you? Because He not only loves you, but He is *in love* with you and wants you to be in love with Him. He wants to be the total and complete love of your life. When you think about Him, you smile; when you've been with Him, you're glowing. Your days of crying are over; start rejoicing that your love life is on track!

You are beautiful, no matter how you feel. There is nothing wrong with you. So what, that relationship that you thought would last for all eternity is now over. But let's talk truthfully, is it over because there's something wrong with you or because there's something wrong with it. How many of us asked God at the beginning of the relationship before we were so emotionally involved that we could not even hear His answer, God is he the one? Let's be honest, most of us married men that God did not tell us to, or if it was the right person, we married in the wrong season. So now we are convinced, "There is something definitely wrong with me."

No, you are beautiful; there is nothing wrong with you. The beauty that we all have no matter what shape or size we are, is from within. Reach deep down on the inside and discover once again just how beautiful you are. However, you have to start exploring who you are as a person. I remember the first time that my children went to visit their father for the summer. I was lost. I didn't know what to do with myself. I had no one to take care of; I felt as if he was taking my life away from me. My very breath was leaving me just thinking about it. The girls were going to be gone for six weeks. What was I going to do? Someone asked me,

"What kinds of things did you like to do?" I didn't even know.

I had built my whole life around taking care of my children that I had no clue about Katina. So, I began to ask myself what I liked to do. I learned that I liked to exercise, get pedicures, read, and most of all, and I enjoyed spending time with my Father, God. God and I really became one during this time; it's amazing how we will even use our children as an excuse not to spend time with God. I had almost let my children take the place that I had once given to my husband. God has to remain first.

Prayer Starter:

Lord Jesus, I thank you that I am fearfully and wonderfully made. My heart trusts in you. Lord put me on a path of righteousness and wholeness. In Jesus' name!

Devotional Scriptures:

John 5:8

Jesus saith unto Him, Rise, take up thy bed, and walk (King James Version)

Isaiah 43:18

But forget all that – it is nothing compared to what I am going to do. (New Living Translation)

2 Corinthians 5:17

This means that anyone who belongs to Christ; he is a new creation. The old has passed away; behold, the new has come. (New Living Translation)

Reflection Questions:

1. **Do you think you are beautiful? Why or Why not?**

_____

_____

_____

_____

_____

2. **Are you still crying about what could have been?**

_____

_____

_____

_____

3. **Is God in His rightful place in your life?**

_____

_____

_____

_____

_____

Journal

_____

_____

_____

_____

_____

_____

_____

_____

_____

_____

_____

_____

_____

_____

_____

_____

_____

_____

_____

_____

_____

_____

CHAPTER SEVEN

God As Father

For many of us a father was not always a significant part in our lives, so we feel like something or someone was missing. It can make us feel incomplete, still searching, wanting to know those little things that we missed out on, wanting answers to all those questions. But I want to share with you today – please let go of your past, for old things are passed away and behold all things become new. You have a great and wonderful father waiting to love you and wrap his arms around you. Even though you are a full-grown woman, it's nothing like having your daddy hug you or say, "Baby girl, everything is going to be alright."

Try this in the middle of chaos, just be still, and put your mind on Father God. Call on your dad; He is right there waiting for you with His arms open wide.

If you need to lay your head on His shoulder, that is available too. Daddy loves His girls. The Word of God asks us if our children are hungry, would we give them a snake? The answer is "no," we want the best for our natural children, so how much more does our heavenly Father love us. You are the apple of His eye. You are His special angel. Whether you make the same mistakes over and over again or you are perfect in everything, your daddy is there waiting for you to acknowledge and receive His love for you.

Many times we search all of our life for that man to love us and provide us with that certain strength, protection, or assurance. We make one wrong choice after another in choosing a mate , looking for this love. Only to one day realize that what we have been saying that our husband or mate was not doing for us was something that we expected from them, but was too great for them to give. They are only to be our mate, not our Father; that particular task can only be filled by the Father.

It is unfair for us to think that our mate can be a father and husband to us at the same time. God is the only one that you are truly looking for, and He is up for the task. The job is not too big. Remember, a true father is not going to turn you away because you had that baby out of wedlock. A true father is not going to turn you away because you married the wrong person. He knew that you were going to make those mistakes. He already figured those into the plan. His love and plan for you have not changed. He is still expecting nothing but the best for you, and expecting you to achieve great things. He is still smiling when He thinks about His baby girl.

YOU are still His baby. A true father corrects and then restores. He will never discipline you and leave you broken and bleeding all over. He will rebuke you and then say now, go ahead and try again. Be healed, my sister, let Father God give you a big hug and assure you that everything will be alright.

KATINA SCOTT

Prayer Starter:

Lord Jesus, I declare you to be my Father. You care about every part of my life; you know exactly how many hairs are on my head. I love you, and I thank you for loving me and teaching me how a father loves a daughter.

Devotional Scriptures:

1 Corinthians 8:6

But for us, there is one God, the Father, by whom all things were created, and for whom we live. And there is one Lord, Jesus Christ, through whom all things were created and through whom we live. (New Living Translation)

Ephesians 4:6

One God and Father of all, who is above all, and through all, and in you all. (Kings James Version)

Isaiah 64:8

But now, O LORD, thou art our Father; we are the clay, and thou our potter, and we all are the work of thy hand (King James Version)

Reflection Questions:

1. Was your relationship with your earthly father a good one?

   _____

   _____

   _____

   _____

2. Do you see God as your father?

   _____

   _____

   _____

   _____

   _____

3. What do you need from Father God at this time in your life?

   _____

   _____

   _____

   _____

   _____

Journal

_____

_____

_____

_____

_____

_____

_____

_____

_____

_____

_____

_____

_____

_____

_____

_____

_____

_____

_____

CHAPTER EIGHT

You Are Strong

D on't forget where you came from-you are stronger than you think. One day I was having a really tough time, and I just began to think about my mom and how she got through tough times in her life. I realized that I am from a line of strong people. The enemy wants you to believe that you are weak and that you can't make it, but that is a lie. The devil is a liar! With my Father not always being in the picture, my mom and I went through some hard times while I was growing up. I didn't always have my mom with me either.

When I was growing up, sometimes we had to be split up so we would both have a place to live. Going through those times as a child made me strong even though I didn't realize it until years later. I was always the child who had to think for myself, take care of myself, and watch out for myself, or at least that's how I felt. So in doing that, there was a strength and determination that was developed inside of me. If God was with me and kept me during those times in my life, why all of a sudden would He leave me now? He is with me in every step that I take, every move I make, God is with me.

The Bible says, *Low I will be with you always even until the end of the world.* Those times helped to build character in me. Now that I'm an adult and when times get hard, sometimes I start to panic and think that I can't make it, what am I going to do? My husband is gone, and how am I going to feed my babies? Well, guess what, I just needed to remember that if God kept me when I was growing up, He was going to keep me now. I am stronger than I think.

The enemy would like for you to think that it's just too hard or that you can't handle this, but why is this situation any different from the last trial that you went through? Looking back, you thought that was going to kill you as well, but you are still standing. God is an awesome God. Hallelujah!!

It's was during this time of my life that I learned confessions were very important. I realized that I needed to declare some things into the atmosphere. I had listened to Satan for many years and repeated the things that he had told me over and over. This was now the time for me to speak some things back to Him.

Don't just take what the enemy is saying to you; it isn't the time to be silent. When He speaks to you, talk back to Him. Learn to fight the right way! The things that were happening were not all what I knew of God and what I knew was ultimately His plan for my life. So, I began to declare some things for my life. The following confessions will help you to walk in victory. I used to have these printed out, and my girls and I read them aloud every day. Read them with me now!

- What Satan means for bad, God means for my good.
- My plan does not always work out, but God is always with me.
- Can't is *not* a word for the believer; I can do all things through Christ who strengthens me. God does not put more on me than I can bear.
- I cannot be defeated; I can do anything that I need to do.
- I agree with my Spirit and not my mind.
- When trouble comes, I calm down; I cannot hear from God when I am upset or in distress.
- When trouble comes, and it will; shake it off.
- My mind is renewed by the Word of God; therefore, I forbid thoughts of failure and defeat to inhabit my mind.

- I have the heart of God, and the heart of God loves the people of God.
- Today grace and peace are my portion.
- All of my needs are met; my storehouses are overflowing.
- Today I receive all of God's blessings and promises for my family and me.
- Today I walk in the complete healing of God.
- Nothing is impossible; with God, all things are possible.
- God is my rock, my fortress, my strong tower, and my deliverer in Him will I trust.

Prayer Starter:

Lord Jesus, my future is bright and promising. I trust you to know what is best for me. You have my best interest at heart. I speak and declare God's word over my life. I love you

Devotional Scriptures:

Proverbs 18:21

Words can bring death or life! Talk too much, and you will eat everything you say. (Contemporary English Version)

Philippians 4:8

Finally brethren whatsoever things are true whatsoever things are honest whatsoever things are just, whatsoever things are pure, whatsoever things are lovely, whatsoever things are of good report; if there be any virtue, and if there be any praise, think on these things (Kings James Version)

Isaiah 55:11

So also will be the Word that I speak—it will not fail to do what I plan for it; it will do everything I send it to do. (Good News Translation)

Reflection Questions:

1. Do I have negative or positive thoughts speaking to you on a daily basis?

    _____

    _____

    _____

    _____

2. How can changing my self-talk help me on a daily basis?

    _____

    _____

    _____

    _____

    _____

3. What are some positive confessions of your own?

    _____

    _____

    _____

    _____

    _____

Journal

_____

_____

_____

_____

_____

_____

_____

_____

_____

_____

_____

_____

_____

_____

_____

_____

_____

_____

_____

_____

_____

_____

_____

CHAPTER NINE

Spiritual Principles

n Galatians 5:22, it tells us that one of the fruits of the Spirit is joy. Therefore, we should strive for joy and not happiness. Happiness is the state of being happy and is defined by what we have according to the world's standards and our circumstances. It's an emotion that we feel. But joy is not an emotion. Joy is something that we can have whether we have a man in our lives or not. Joy is something we can have, whether we have money in the bank or not. It has nothing to do with the things that we own or how we feel at the time. Joy is knowing that no matter what the need is right now that my God shall supply all my needs according to His riches in glory (Philippians 4:19), so I don't have to walk around upset or despondent. Joy is knowing that all things work together for the good for those who love the Lord and are called according to His purpose (Romans 8:28). The joy of the Lord is our strength. It is our joy in God that keeps us going when facts and situations say that we should buckle in defeat.

Another thing that I learned, which was very important was the Spirit of truth. The Spirit of truth is simply this: the facts of the situation may not be very good – you may go to the doctor, and he may say that you have Cancer – the Spirit of truth says that you shall live and not die; the Spirit of truth says that by His stripes we are healed. Speak truth to every situation. Speaking truth is speaking the mind of Christ, it's speaking hope to a dead situation, it's speaking faith instead of fear, it's speaking love instead of hate. I encourage you, my sister, to speak the truth to that situation that you are in right now. The enemy says that you will always be in this situation that you will never be delivered or free. But the Spirit of truth says that for whom the Son sets free He is free indeed. The enemy says that you will always be broke, you will never have enough. The Spirit of truth says that I have more than enough and that my God shall supply all my needs according to His riches in Glory, (Philippians 4:13). The Spirit of truth unlocks us from the place of bondage that the enemy has our mind and emotions. God's truth is illuminated by His Word being made manifest in our lives. The Word of God is life, and there is life in the Word. The first time that I had to speak at our singles meeting this is the message that God gave to me to share. The Word has to become a part of our daily life. In John 1:1, it says that in the beginning was the Word and the Word was with God, and the Word was God.

Prayer Starter:

Lord Jesus, before anything was formed, your Word was. Your Word spoke everything into existence. Teach me your ways and principles, teach me your words. Lord, write them on the tables of my heart. Lord, help me to follow your ways, so I will live the life that you have for me. In Jesus' name!

Devotional Scriptures:

1 Corinthians 13:7

Love never gives up, never loses faith, is always hopeful, and endures through every circumstance. (New Living Translation)

Hebrews 13:8

Jesus Christ is the same yesterday, and today, and forever. (New Living Translation)

John 1:1

In the beginning was the Word, and the Word was with God, and the Word was God. (New International Version)

Reflection Questions:

1. What promises can you find in the Word of God?

    _____

    _____

    _____

    _____

    _____

2. Are these promises only for a select few or for us all?

    _____

    _____

    _____

    _____

    _____

3. How does God's Word come alive in your life
    everyday?

    _____

    _____

    _____

    _____

    _____

Journal

_____

_____

_____

_____

_____

_____

_____

_____

_____

_____

_____

_____

_____

_____

_____

_____

_____

_____

_____

CHAPTER TEN

Steps To Emotional Freedom

t is possible for the pain to end. The day that I realized that I was free when I awoke, it was just another day. I went through that day as normal as any other, but later that evening, the phone rang. I answered the phone, and it was my ex-husband, we exchanged pleasantries, and he asked for the girls because He wanted to tell them He had gotten married. I handed the phone to my daughter, and at that moment, I realized that I wasn't hurting. My daughter was upset, but I could have shouted. I had just found out that the person whom I would have done anything in this world for, had just joined Himself with someone else and my heart did not hurt. I declare to you today that God's Word is true. The Word of God is healing and freeing of our past and gives us hope for our future.

God wants to do a quick work in his people. . Healing and restoration are available to us right now. It all starts with our obedience to his word. He doesn't have time for us to take a 12-month course or take baby steps. God needs us to go by leaps and bounds. God needs us to run, not walk. Other people are waiting for us to be free, so we must learn to take God at His Word. Every Word of God is true, and as you get into the Word each day, you will begin to walk in freedom.

You must find a ministry to join and become committed to. Every time we had a service, midweek or Sunday, I found myself in the church. I didn't want to miss anything. With each service, I grew stronger and stronger. In Ephesians 4:16, the Bible tells us that every joint supplies. We all need each other to grow and live.

Consecration and prayer were instrumental in my healing process. Consecration is not just something for those people of old or for "holy rollers," but Consecration is a necessary part of our Christian walk: to separate yourselves from the things of this world and to focus on God and the things of God. This is necessary.

Remember what Word that God has promised you. We all have words and promises that God has made to us. Hold on to those words and rehearse them every day. God's Word is true, and He will fulfill it. God's Word will accomplish everything that it was sent out to do and will not return unto Him void.

Prayer Starter

Lord Jesus, I need you. I need your guidance and direction. Lead me to a ministry that will help me to grow and learn more of you. Lord help me to be free so I can help others be free.

Devotional Scripture

John 8:36

So if the Son sets you free, you are truly free. (New Living Translation)

Galatians 5:1

Stand fast therefore in the liberty wherewith Christ hath made us free, and be not entangled again with the yoke of bondage. (King James Version)

Romans 6:23

When people sin, they earn what sin pays—death. But God gives His people a free gift—eternal life in Christ Jesus, our Lord. (Easy-to-Read Version)

Reflection Questions

1. **Are you ready to experience the freedom that God has for you?**

   _____

   _____

   _____

2. **What is your number one prayer request before God right now?**

   _____

   _____

   _____

3. **What words/promises has God spoken over your life?**

   _____

   _____

   _____

Journal

_____

_____

_____

_____

_____

_____

_____

_____

_____

_____

_____

_____

_____

_____

_____

_____

_____

_____

_____

_____

_____

_____

_____

_____

CHAPTER ELEVEN

God Really Does Have A Plan
~ It's A Setup

When my husband and I separated, I was devastated. I was so upset with God. But it was all in His plan. My destiny and His purpose were more important than my feelings. It was my husband's decision for us to move to Delaware, and at the time, my mother and two of my sisters were there, so he said I would have some family members close to me. As a result, reluctantly, I moved to Delaware.

Have you ever been in a place and hated even the look and smell of it? Everything about it made me mad. I remember being in the nursery one day at church feeding my baby and my first lady saying to me, "God says that you are going to be here for a while, so don't plan on leaving anytime soon." I became so angry. Why? I didn't want to stay. Of course, there was nothing that I could do, because the girls and I did not have anywhere else that we could go.

We began to settle down in DE, and then the unthinkable happened, my family left DE and the girls, and I were left alone. God was trying to tell me that He wanted to be my focus. He wanted to be my love, He wanted to be first in my life. I had to learn to cleave to God like my life depended on it because guess what? It did. God had a plan all along for us to be here, and my divorce was only a setup to fulfill God's plan, the vehicle that He used to get us here. But why did He have to use a divorce and have me go through all that pain? I'm glad you asked. One day I asked Him myself. He responded to me that I would not have learned any other way.

What was I learning? I was learning how to love God. I was learning how to trust God. I was learning how to have a relationship with someone who really cared about me. As deep as my hurt and pain were, God's love is just as deep. I had to learn that He does have a plan and that He does love me. Remember that God is not concerned about our emotions; only His will being fulfilled in the earth. When we have gotten ourselves into situations that He did not even tell us to get into, He has to break us out of that so we can fulfill His purpose in our lives.

Prayer Starter:

Lord Jesus, I realize that you have a plan and purpose for my life. I'm ready to experience this new relationship with you. Help me to trust you and lean on you through this process.

Devotional Scripture:

Jeremiah 29:11

For I know the plans I have for you," declares the LORD, "plans to prosper you and not to harm you, plans to give you hope and a future. (New International Version)

I Timothy 2:3-4

For this is good and acceptable in the sight of God our Saviour; [4] Who will have all men to be saved, and to come unto the knowledge of the truth. (King James Version)

I Thessalonians 5:18

In everything give thanks: for this is the will of God in Christ Jesus concerning you. (King James Version)

Reflection Questions:

1. **Do you believe that God has a plan for your life?**

   _____

   _____

   _____

2. **Do you believe that God wants the best for you? Why or why not?**

   _____

   _____

   _____

3. **Do you know what God's best is for you? Are you ready to experience it?**

   _____

   _____

   _____

   _____

Journal

_____

_____

_____

_____

_____

_____

_____

_____

_____

_____

_____

_____

_____

_____

_____

_____

_____

_____

_____

_____

_____

_____

Conclusion

Be free my sisters, be free mothers and be free my friends. Walk in the freedom of God. The Word of God says that I wish above all things that ye shall prosper and be in good health even as your soul prospers (John 4:34). Don't quit. Don't give up. Don't look back. Though the pain is real and severe, **it is not unto death.** The end of a thing is far better than the beginning (Ecclesiastes 7:8). Your future is so much better than anything or anyone that you had to leave behind or give up. It may hurt, but believe me, it was the best thing for your life. No good thing will He withhold from you. Don't give up. Everything that you need is before you, not behind you. Everything is alright. Let out your cry, go ahead, and scream, but know that God hears all, and He sees all. Your tears He's bottled up. He is right there.

Every day you will need to make up your mind that you will accept God's plan and will for your life and not Satan's. At times you will see that your biggest enemy is yourself. You will need to continually walk in God's love and grace for your life.

Don't accept what life offers you. God has so much for you. Run with the vision that He sets before you.

There is life after death. Why do I say this? Because when you have experienced something very traumatic in your life, you feel like you are going to die if not actually dying due to all the chaos that you go through. It's time to let the healing process begin. There is no set time for us to be healed. God has everyone on a different timeline. For me, the healing process was years. But for you, God wants to do a quick work! Be open to Him changing you in spite of your past and your life.

Victory

The last part of this book that I want to share with you is simple but, most importantly, the Word of God. As I stated earlier, the Word of God is life to us. When we are deficient in God's Word, we are weak and easily distracted from what is important in life and for us. But when we are full of the Word, we are strong. Now, don't think that you have to memorize all these scriptures. But look at these healing scriptures and find some that speak to you directly. Those are the ones that I would encourage you to hide in your heart, hold them close and say them over and over. They will help you rebuild your life. Take one day at a time, small baby steps. You don't have to try to conquer it all in one day. But just know that this is your time of breakthrough, renewal, and restoration. God is going to give you just what you need. I speak victory to you today! You are victorious already! God knew this moment was going to happen in your life, and He is here to help you handle it.

Now Let's Pray!

Father God in the name of Jesus, I take this time now to hold my sister before you, Lord. Today I am her voice. Give her strength where she has none. Give her hope where she has none. Give her a heart and mind to forgive her transgressor Lord and also to forgive herself. Lord open up her heart right now in the name of Jesus. Lord, tear down the walls of stone that have been built up by years of hurt, anger, unforgiveness, and doubt. Lord, give her a heart of flesh. Lord, I command my sister to be free, to receive you and your healing into her heart.

Lord God, I speak complete and total freedom from every emotional holdup, any person, or any vice that she may have in her life. Father, I rebuke every devil that comes against your Word and her freedom, and I plead the blood of Jesus over my sister and her seed, for the blood covers, the blood protects, the blood cleanses us of all transgressions, Lord. Father, fill my sister with your love; let her experience your true love in the name of Jesus. Now rise up, take up thy bed and walk. Walk in the freedom and liberty of Christ Jesus. In the name of Jesus, I pray!

Amen!

Healing Scriptures

Psalm 34:18
The Lord is nigh unto them that are of a broken heart; and saveth such as be of a contrite spirit.

Proverbs 3:5-6
Trust in the Lord with all thine heart; and lean not unto thine own understanding.

Psalms 127:3
Lo, children are a heritage of the Lord; and the fruit of the womb is hishisHis reward.

Psalms 73:26
My flesh and my heart faileth: but God is the strength of my heart and my portion forever.

Revelation 21:4
And God shall wipe away all tears from their eyes, and there shall be no more death, neither sorrow nor crying, neither shall there be any more pain: for the former things are passed away.

Isaiah 41:10
Fear thou not, for I am with thee: be not dismayed; for I am thy God: I will strengthen thee; yea, I will help thee; yea, I will uphold thee with the right hand of my righteousness.

I Corinthians 13:7
Beareth all things, believieth all things, hopeth all things, endureth all things.

John 14:27
Peace I leave with you, my peace I give unto you: not as the world giveth, give I unto you. Let not your heart be troubled, neither let it be afraid.

Psalms 55:22
Cast thy burden upon the Lord, and He shall sustain thee: He shall never suffer the righteous to be moved.

2 Corinthians 12:9
And He said unto me, My grace is sufficient for thee: for my strength is made perfect in weakness. Most gladly, therefore, will I rather glory in my infirmities. That the power of Christ may rest upon me.

2 Corinthians 5:7
For we walk by faith, not by sight

Matthew 11:28-30
Come unto me all ye that labour and are heavy laden, and I will give you rest.

Hebrews 13:8
Jesus Christ the same yesterday, and today, and forever

1 Peter 2:24
Who has his own self bare our sins in His body on the tree, that we, being dead to sins, should live unto righteousness: by whose stripes ye were healed.

John 14:13
And whatsoever ye shall ask in my name, that will I do, that the Father may be glorified in the Son
Mark 11:23 – for verily I say unto you, That whatsoever shall say unto this mountain, Be thou removed and be thou cast in to the sea; and shall not doubt in His heart, but shall believe that those things which He saith shall come to pass; He shall have whatsoever He saith

Hebrews 11:1
Now faith is the substance of things hoped for, the evidence of things not seen

Romans 12:2
And be not conformed to this world; but be ye transformed by the renewing of your mind, that ye may prove what is that good, and acceptable and perfect will of God.

I Peter 4:19
Wherefore let them that suffer according to the will of God commit the keeping of their souls to Him in well-doing, as unto a faithful creator.
Psalms 107:20

He sent His word, and healed them, and delivered them from their destructions.

2 Corinthians 12:7-10
And lest I should be exalted above measure through the abundance of the revelations, there was given to me a thorn in the flesh, the messenger of Satan to buffet me, lest I should be exalted above measure.

Matthew 17:20
And Jesus said unto them, Because of your unbelief: for verily I say unto you, If ye have faith as a grain of mustard seed, ye shall say unto this mountain, Remove hence to yonder place; and it shall remove, and nothing shall be impossible unto you.

Romans 8:28
And we know that all things work together for good to them that love God, to them who are the called according to His purpose.

Psalms 41:4
I said Lord be merciful unto me: heal my soul; for I have sinned against thee.

I Corinthians 10:13
There hath o temptation taken you but such as is common to man; but God is faithful, who will not suffer you to be tempted above that ye are able, but will with the temptation also make a way of escape, that ye may be able to bear it.

1 Corinthians 6:19-20
What? Know ye not that your body is the temple of the Holy Ghost which is in you, which ye have of God and ye are not your own?

Ephesians 6:13
Wherefore take unto you the whole armour of God, that ye may be able to withstand in the evil day, and having done all, to stand.

Hebrews 11:6
But without faith, it is impossible to please Him: for He that cometh to God must believe that He is, and that He is a rewarder of them that diligently seek Him.

John 10:10
The thief cometh not, but for to steal, and to kill, and to destroy: I am come that they might have life and that they might have it more abundantly.

Psalms 103:3
Who forgiveth all thine iniquities; who healeth all thy diseases;

Philippians 4:13
I can do all things through Christ, which strengtheneth me.

3 John 1:2
Beloved, I wish above all things that thou mayest prosper and be in health, even as thy soul prospereth.

Romans 10:17
So then faith [cometh] by hearing, and hearing by the Word of God.

John 3:16
For God so loved the world, that He gave His only begotten Son, that whosoever believeth in Him should not perish, but have everlasting life.

Isaiah 53:5
But He was wounded for our transgressions, He was bruised for our iniquities: the chastisement of our peace [was] upon Him, and with His stripes we are healed.

Psalms 23:1-6
The LORD is my shepherd; I shall not want.

Psalms 27:13-14
I had fainted unless I had believed to see the goodness of the LORD in the land of the living. Wait on the LORD: be of good courage, and He shall strengthen thine heart: wait, I say, on the LORD.

Deuteronomy 31:6
Be strong and of good courage, fear not, nor be afraid of them: for the LORD thy God, He [it is] that doth go with thee; He will not fail thee, nor forsake thee.

John 14:12
Verily, verily, I say unto you, He that believeth on me, the works that I do shall He do also, and greater works than these shall He do; because I go unto my Father.

Exodus 15:26
And said, If thou wilt diligently hearken to the voice of the LORD thy God, and wilt do that which is right in His sight, and wilt give ear to His commandments and keep all His statutes, I will put none of these diseases upon thee, which I have brought upon the Egyptians: for I am the LORD that healeth thee.

Philippians 3:13
Brethren, I count not myself to have apprehended: but this one thing I do, forgetting those things which are behind, and reaching forth unto those things which are before,

John 1:1
In the beginning, was the Word, and the Word was with God, and the Word was God.

Romans 8:1
There is therefore now no condemnation to them which are in Christ Jesus, who walk not after the flesh, but after the Spirit.

Isaiah 43:18
Remember ye not the fo1mer things, neither consider the things of old.

Mark 16:17-18
And these signs shall follow them that believe; In my name shall they cast out devils; they shall speak with new tongues

Psalms 56:8
Thou tellest my wanderings: put thou my tears into thy bottle: are they not in thy book?

Malachi 3:6
For I am the LORD, I change not; therefore, ye sons of Jacob are not consumed.

Psalms 118:1-18
Oh give thanks unto the LORD; for He is good: because His mercy endureth forever.

Romans 6:23
For the wages of sin is death; but the gift of God is eternal life through Jesus Christ our Lord.

Acts 3:6
Then Peter said, Silver and gold have I none; but such as I have give I thee: In the name of Jesus Christ of Nazareth 1ise up and walk.

Mark 16:18
They shall take up serpents; and if they drink any deadly thing, it shall not hurt them; they shall lay hands on the sick, and they shall recover.

1 John 4:16

And we have known and believed the love that God hath to us. God is love; and He that dwelleth in love dwelleth in God, and God in Him.

Lamentations 3:22

It is of the LORD'S mercies that we are not consumed, because His compassions fail not.

John 1:14

And the Word was made flesh, and dwelt among us, (and we beheld His glory, the glory as of the only begotten of the Father,) full of grace and truth.

Luke 12:2

For there is nothing covered, that shall not be revealed; neither hid, that shall not be known.

Philippians 3:13-14

Brethren, I count not myself to have apprehended: but [this] one thing [I do], forgetting those things which are behind, and reaching forth unto those things which are before,

2 Thessalonians 2:16-17

Now our Lord Jesus Christ Himself, and God, even our Father, which hath loved us, and hath given [us] everlasting consolation and good hope through grace,

Hebrews 12:1

Wherefore seeing we also are compassed about with so great a cloud of witnesses, let us lay aside every weight, and the sin which doth so easily beset [us], and let us run with patience the race that is set before us,

Psalms 91:1

He that dwelleth in the secret place of the Most High shall abide under the shadow of the Almighty.

Psalms 63:1-11

0 God, thou [art] my God; early will I seek thee: my soul thirsteth for thee, my flesh longeth for thee in a dry and thirsty laud, where no water is;

Hosea 13:14

I will ransom them from the power of the grave; I will redeem them from death: death, I will be thy plagues; grave, I will be thy destruction: repentance shall be hid from mine eyes.

Matthew 8:16-17

When the even was come, they brought unto Him many that were possessed with devils: and He cast out the spirits with [His] Word, and healed all that were sick:

Matthew 14:31

And immediately, Jesus stretched forth [His] hand, and caught Him, and said unto Him, O thou of little faith, wherefore didst thou doubt?

Hebrews 2:4
God also bearing [them] witness, both with signs and wonders, and with divers miracles, and gifts of the Holy Ghost, according to His own will?

Romans 5:2
By whom also we have access by faith into His grace wherein we stand, and rejoice in the hope of the glory of God.

2 Corinthians 12:12
Truly, the signs of an apostle were wrought among you in all patience, in signs, and wonders, and mighty deeds.

Acts 19:11-12
And God wrought special miracles by the hands of Paul:

Matthew 10:1
And when He had called unto Him His twelve disciples, He gave them power against unclean spirits, to cast them out, and to heal all manner of sickness and all manner of disease.

1 John 4:1-21
Beloved, believe not every Spirit, but try the spirits whether they are of God: because many false prophets are gone out into the world.

Luke 4:18
The Spirit of the Lord is upon me, because He hath anointed me to preach the gospel to the poor; He hath sent me to heal the brokenhearted, to preach deliverance to the captives, and

recovering of sight to the blind, to set at liberty them that are bruised.

Isaiah 30:26
Moreover the light of the moon shall be as the light of the sun, and the light of the sun shall be sevenfold, as the light of seven days, in the day that the LORD bindeth up the breach of hishisHis people, and healeth the stroke of their wound.

Psalms 62:1-12
Truly my soul waiteth upon God: from Him cometh my salvation.

Philippians 4:6-7
Be careful for nothing; but in everything by prayer and supplication with thanksgiving, let your requests be made known unto God.

Matthew 8:1-34
When He was come down from the mountain, great multitudes followed Him.

Habakkuk 3:16-19
When I heard, my belly trembled; my lips quivered at the voice: rottenness entered into my bones, and I trembled in myself, that I might rest in the day of trouble: when He cometh up unto the people, He will invade them with hishisHis troops.

Acts 14:8-10
And there sat a certain man at Lystra, impotent in His feet, being a cripple from His mother's womb, who never had walked:

Proverbs 17:17
A friend loveth at all times, and a brother is born for adversity.

John 11:1-57
Now a certain man was sick, named Lazarus, of Bethany, the town of Mary and her sister Martha.

Luke 13:11-13
And, behold, there was a woman which had a spirit of infirmity eighteen years, and was bowed together, and could in no wise lift up herself.

Matthew 24:1-51
And Jesus went out, and departed from the temple: and His disciples came to Him for the buildings of the temple.

Matthew 9:1-38
And He entered into a ship, and passed over, and came into His own city.

Hosea 2:14-15
Therefore, behold, I will allure her, and bring her into the wilderness, and speak comfortably unto her.

Acts 17:11

These were more noble than those in Thessalonica, in that they received the Word with all readiness of mind, and searched the scriptures daily, whether those things were so.

Proverbs 1:20

Wisdom crieth without; she uttereth Her voice in the streets:

Jude 1:3

Beloved, when I gave all diligence to write unto you of the common salvation, it was needful for me to write unto you, and exhort you that ye should earnestly contend for the faith which was once delivered unto the saints.

Acts 14:3

Long time, therefore, abode they speaking boldly in the Lord, which gave testimony unto the Word of His grace, and granted signs and wonders to be done by their hands.

Acts 2:22

Ye men of Israel, hear these words; Jesus of Nazareth, a man approved of God among you by miracles and wonders and signs, which God did by Him in the midst of you, as ye yourselves also know:

Luke 9:1

Then He called His twelve disciples together, and gave them power and authority over all devils, and to cure diseases.

Isaiah 1:1-31
The vision of Isaiah the Son of Amoz, which He saw concerning Judah and Jerusalem in the days of Uzziah, Jotham, Ahaz, and Hezekiah, kings of Judah.

Isaiah 61:1-3
The Spirit of the Lord GOD is upon me; because the LORD hath anointed me to preach good tidings unto the meek; He hath sent me to bind up the brokenhearted, to proclaim liberty to the captives, and the opening of the prison to them that are bound;

Joshua 1:7-8
Only be thou strong and very courageous, that thou mayest observe to do according to all the law, which Moses my servant commanded thee: tum not from it to the right hand or to the left, that thou mayest prosper whithersoever thou goest.

Song of Solomon 1:1-17
the song of songs, which is Solomon's.

Psalms 119:16-17
I will delight myself in thy statutes: I will not forget thy Word.

Psalms 34:17-18
The righteous cry, and the LORD heareth, and delivereth them out of all their troubles.

1 Corinthians 13:4-7

Charity suffereth long, and is kind; charity envieth not; charity vaunteth not itself, is not puffed up,

Hosea 14:4-8

I will heal their backsliding, I will love them freely: for mine anger is turned away from Him.

Hosea 6:3

Then shall we know, if we follow on to know the LORD: His going forth is prepared as the morning; and He shall come unto us as the rain, as the latter and former rain unto the earth.

Psalms 61:1

Hear my cry, Oh God; attend unto my prayer.
All scriptures in this chapter taken from King James Version of the Bible.

www.ingramcontent.com/pod-product-compliance
Lightning Source LLC
Chambersburg PA
CBHW060338130626
46553CB00003B/1042